HANDICAPPING
THE WALL STREET WAY

HANDICAPPING
THE WALL STREET WAY

Picking *Xtra Winners* at the Track

MARK E. RIPPLE

Lexington, Kentucky

Library of Congress Control Number: 2005920845

ISBN-13: 978-1-58150-126-1
ISBN-10: 1-58150-126-9

Printed in the United States of America
First Edition: 2005

Distributed to the trade by
National Book Network
4501 Forbes Blvd., Suite 200, Lanham, MD 20706
1.800.462.6420

A Division of
Blood-Horse Publications
Publishers Since 1916

Contents

To my wife:
Thanks, Terri, for putting up with me

E.C.D.: "Cat's in the Cradle"

B.A.R.: "Greatest comeback in Travers history"

Thinking "Outside-the-Box"

This book is going to force you to think "outside-the-box." By that I mean you will be compelled to re-examine your faith in everything that you have read about handicapping. After doing so, you will realize that yesterday's methods do not necessarily work today and have less of a chance of working tomorrow. Because you purchased this book, you obviously have no immediate intention of quitting the game and are what I consider to be a serious handicapper. Therefore, you are constantly looking for new ways to improve your handicapping and when faced with the possibility that you are handicapping with outdated methods and beliefs, you know that your only recourse is to change your strategy. Don't be afraid. Change is good.

I've studied and mastered just about every handicapping method available today. When I realized that by and large these methods were not highly reliable and when they did work, they only produced a very small profit margin, I began to search for another way. I began to think "outside-the box." I have the double fortune of a highly advanced understanding of both handicapping and the stock market. When I realized just how easily my knowledge of the stock market lent itself to my love of handicapping, I knew I had to develop a method of handicapping that incorporated market theory with handicapping. I did and have been successful with this method for years. Let me share with you my method, and I promise you will not be disappointed.

Efficient Market Hypothesis

The Model for the Efficient Pool Hypothesis

My approach to handicapping closely resembles the approach to investing of the great contrarian investor, David Dreman. He is the author of such investor classics as *Contrarian Investment Strategy* and *Psychology and the Stock Market*. Dreman is known for going against the crowd and investing in companies that are out of favor. I studied Dreman back in the late eighties (when I was a stockbroker) and melded some of his investment theories with my own handicapping strategies to create a unique and powerful way to play the horses.

Navigating the seemingly opposite and intricate worlds of Wall Street and the racetrack for financial gain can be tricky, yet many of the principles can be extrapolated from one to the other. Imagine hiring a chimpanzee to manage your money. It sounds insane, doesn't it? Well, in 1993, the Swedish newspaper *Expressen* gave five stock analysts and a chimpanzee named Ola $1,250 each in "play" money to see how much they could earn in the stock market. While the so-called experts carefully analyzed their selections, Ola practiced her dart-throwing skills using the Stockholm stock pages from *Expressen*'s business section as her target. The contest ran for one month, and Ola won.

The point of the contest was to illustrate the theory that at any given moment a stock's price is the best measure of its value and analysts' efforts to discover undervalued stocks are useless. This theory is the basis for the Efficient Market Hypothesis (EMH). The EMH was first put forth by Eugene Fama, a giant in the field of economics in the 1960s and '70s.

The EMH argues that stocks are never undervalued because investors labor so hard at uncovering them. This hypothesis assumes that all relevant data affecting the price of a stock are recognized and continuously examined by investors. Because this information is immediately assessed, the EMH concludes that all stocks must be efficiently priced, especially ones such as IBM, a core holding in many mutual fund portfolios.

While Fama's theory holds true some of the time, it is also based upon certain assumptions that do not always hold true. David Dreman is able to recognize situations where stocks are not efficiently priced and subsequently invest in those companies he deems undervalued. I take the same approach to handicapping and try to identify horses that are overlays or have odds high enough to offer a better-than-average return for the risk of making a bet. This is how we handicappers make our money. In order for you to better grasp this concept, I will continue to draw parallels between the stock market and the pari-mutuel "market" or betting pool.

As handicappers, we find value plays in horses the general public overlooks. These horses can be said to have inefficient odds. Most of us call them overlays. By studying the parallels between the stock market and pari-mutuel "market" or betting pool, we gain new insight in how to discover inefficiencies in the betting pool. Discovering these inefficiencies will aid us in our quest for value plays on overlays at the racetrack. The story of Ola is comparable to someone sticking a needle through the eye of the cover horse on a program and selecting every equine whose name the needle happens to puncture. While we handicappers spend countless hours examining past performance lines in order to predict the outcome of a race, sometimes at the end of an unsuccessful day we feel that our return on investment could have been markedly higher had we used a needle. It's a frustrating feeling for sure, and one that may lead us to draw a wrong conclusion. We could conclude that our attempts to discover value are pointless because at any given moment a horse's odds reflect its true chances. This is wrong! In a June 2000 article for *American Turf Monthly*, I wrote about the Efficient Market Hypothesis (EMH). In order to keep this book in handicapping terms, I am substituting Efficient Pool Hypothesis for the Efficient Market Hypothesis. Don't get bogged down with these terms. We are really exploring here the forces that cause inefficiencies in the betting pool and thus lead us to value plays or overlays.

Efficient Pool Hypothesis

Let's assume, for argument's sake, that what I said about IBM is true: No less than seventeen analysts constantly analyze the stock, 95 percent of which is owned by institutions and mutual funds. IBM is an efficiently priced stock and nobody (in present day) is going to get rich quick from investing in it. A fair comparison would be to call Secretariat the IBM of horses. It's doubtful that any handicapper ever got rich by betting on him. Secretariat was hardly an overlay. There are hundreds of horses and stocks of which we have never heard, or that are out of favor, with the potential to make the astute investor or handicapper big money. They can be called inefficient, meaning that their odds and prices do not reflect their true value at any given moment. Therefore, it is essential for the handicapper or investor to be able to recognize these undervalued commodities. In order to understand how to find horses with inefficient odds, we must first examine the fundamental elements of what I call the Efficient Pool Hypothesis:

1. There are no true overlays for the sole reason that horseplayers labor so hard at uncovering them.
2. All relevant data affecting the odds of a horse are recognized by handicappers.

3. All relevant data affecting the odds of a horse are continuously examined by handicappers.

4. All horses must have efficient odds, thereby reflecting all the facts, beliefs, and predictions that impact any given horse's chances of winning.

Finding the flaws in this hypothesis will enable you to identify races and horses that are most likely to produce inefficient odds.

The Flaws of Both the EMH and EPH

Fear

Fear can become a dominant influence on stock prices or odds whenever investors or handicappers abandon rational thinking in favor of crowd psychology. If an investor is averse to risk, he or she may sell a stock too hastily if it begins to drop in price. For example, on October 19, 2004, an Associated Press article subtitled "Delta Airlines Will Report Huge Loss for Third Quarter Amid Fears of Bankruptcy Filing" prompted many irrational investors to sell. The next day Delta's share price closed at $2.93, down 8 percent from $3.24. (The price had been as high as $9.12 on March 1, 2004.) Just twenty-three days later the pilots' union agreed to reduce salaries and concede raises for the next five years. On November 19, 2004, Delta's share price closed at $6.60. That's a 125 percent return on investment in one month! Those investors who had panicked over the words "loss" and "bankruptcy" and immediately sold their stock, thinking to get out while the stock still had some value, caused the price of the stock to fall. But had the stock's value really changed or had fear changed the perception of the stock's value? When subsequent events ameliorated the severity of the situation, other investors saw the chance to buy the now undervalued stock at a lower price and were rewarded months later with a significant increase in value.

I developed the Last Race Consensus Pick Angle around fear. Fearing a losing day, the general public is sometimes prone to desperate attempts at recovering their losses in the last race. Unsophisticated bettors will discard professional thinking and take a big gamble on a longshot. The result of many players betting a longshot is twofold: The longshot will almost assuredly become an underlay, while more solid horses, the *Daily Racing Form*'s consensus pick for example, will become overlays.

The professional handicapper should take careful note when longshots have dominated a day's card. In such instances, it can be assumed the preponderance of handicappers will have been losing all afternoon. Consequently, in the last race they will be trying extremely hard to break even by betting the remainder of their bankroll on a longshot. Again, this situation is most prevalent upon arrival of the day's last race. Provided that the last race is not a cheap claiming race or a race for two-year-olds, which are races typical to the second half of the late double, the true professionals who have not gone home can exploit this phenomenon by simply playing the *DRF*'s consensus selection. We already know about widely followed stocks and horses. Because the *DRF* is a widely read paper, its selection will usually go off as an overbet favorite with odds so low it puts us in a maximum risk/minimum return situation — one we want to avoid. However, when fear of a losing day sweeps through the majority of bettors, it tilts the scales, and the odds on the *DRF* consensus selection can become elevated to the point where we are once again in a minimum risk/maximum return situation.

On November 7, 2004, Delaware Park hosted the Arabian Cup Championship Sprint, a grade I stakes race for Arabian horses three years old and up. It was the tenth and last race on Delaware's card.

NAME	MORNING LINE ODDS	POST TIME ODDS	FINISH
Ontario	3-1 DRF consensus pick	9-2	1st
All Tu Kool	4-1	6-1	4th
No Show Jones	5-1	7-1	3rd
Th Richie	**6-1**	**1-1***	**2nd**
Tri Traveller	6-1	29-1	6th
Sudden Mischief	6-1	7-1	5th
Doc Toothman	10-1	8-1	9th
Eagle One	15-1	85-1	7th
Noble House	20-1	48-1	8th

While I wasn't too keen on playing a sprint race with this angle, the quality of the horses entered was enough to persuade me. An avalanche of desperate money poured down on Th Richie, depressing the horse's odds from 6-1 to even money. My guess is this happened because he was trained by Philip E. Saxer Jr., the trainer in that race with the highest winning percentage. Looking at the results, you can see that the odds on the *DRF* consensus pick (and the morning-line favorite), Ontario, gently floated upward from 3-1 to 9-2. My $18 win bet on Ontario returned $100.80.

Greed-Induced Euphoria

Greed-induced euphoria or exaggerated elation is another tremendous influence on both the stock market and betting pool. In a long and powerful market advance, similar to the one that ended in 1999 with the burst of the technology sector's bubble, investors tend to abandon rational thinking because of the temptation of large and instant profits. During the technology sector boom, the prices on those kinds of stocks rose to levels their earnings could not support. Everybody who owned stock in the technology sector was making money. Technology stocks became the "get rich quick" fad of the moment, and no portfolio was complete without them. Soon, people who didn't own them began to doubt their own intelligence, so, in spite of the large quarterly losses that many of these companies were reporting, they bought, no matter the cost in relation to the true value, and prices continued to rise. But once investors saw faulty business plans fueling quarterly losses that far contradicted the rising stock prices, they became disenchanted and beat a hasty retreat. The mass exodus burst the technology stock bubble and left many people broke. The inefficiency here was caused by investors paying more than something was worth. These inefficiencies can also occur in horse racing when even serious bettors get caught up in greed-induced euphoria.

After a horse has won the first two legs of the Triple Crown, many of the most disciplined professionals join the frenzied betting on the sentimental favorite in the Belmont Stakes instead of betting intelligently. We look no further than Smarty Jones in the 2004 Belmont to see that this is true. Granted, the 1-5 favorite, Smarty Jones, was a fantastic horse. He had won the Kentucky Derby and Preakness in fine fashion. Folks began to adopt a "he can't lose" attitude, and he became one of the hippest horses in history. Otherwise rational players doubted their own intelligence and bet Smarty only because they didn't want to be left out. However, Marylou Whitney's Birdstone, at 36-1 and with Edgar Prado aboard, passed the fatigued Smarty Jones as the finish line drew near, winning by one length.

Knowing that the odds on Smarty were wildly depressed, thereby creating inefficiencies and overlays elsewhere, I opted to spread my risk among two or more wagers, an approach known as dutching. Dutching also allows the handicapper to predetermine the net profit of the collective wagers. Desiring to reward myself one thousand dollars for the risk, I placed these wagers:

OUTLAY	TYPE OF BET	HORSE	FINISH	ODDS	PAYOFF
$22	Win	Caiman	8th	49-1	$0
$27	Win	Tap Dancer	6th	40-1	$0
$30	Win	Birdstone	1st	36-1	$1,080

Subtracting my total outlay of $79 from the payoff of $1,080 left me with a net profit of $1,001.

Contrarian thinking is believing the improbable will probably happen. The public, in its greed-induced euphoria, thought it highly improbable that Smarty Jones would not win the Belmont Stakes.

Another great example was Charismatic in the 1999 Belmont Stakes. Again, the crowd's excitement was tangible, becoming contagious. However, most of us know what happened: The odds on Lemon Drop Kid were elevated to 29-1, and he won by a head over Vision and Verse. The 3-2 favorite, Charismatic, settled for third after fracturing his left front leg during the race.

There are many more examples of horses that won the first two legs of the Triple Crown and went off as the favorite in the Belmont Stakes, but did not win. Not including Burgoo King in 1932 and Bold Venture in 1936, both of whom won the Kentucky Derby and the Preakness but did not start in the Belmont Stakes, eighteen have failed to win the Triple Crown after taking the Kentucky Derby and Preakness Stakes.

Why do the horses belonging to this elite group lose in the Belmont Stakes? Various reasons. And, given the statistics, why do these Triple Crown contenders attract so much money? America wants a hero, whether it is a man, woman, or horse. This is euphoria. The betting public desires a Triple Crown winner so much that it is willing to overlook that the grueling

YEAR	HORSE	BELMONT FINISH	WINNER
1944	Pensive	Second	Bounding Home
1958	Tim Tam	Second	Cavan
1961	Carry Back	Seventh	Sherluck
1964	Northern Dancer	Third	Quadrangle
1966	Kauai King	Fourth	Amberoid
1968	Forward Pass	Second	Stage Door Johnny
1969	Majestic Prince	Second	Arts and Letters
1971	Canonero II	Fourth	Pass Catcher
1979	Spectacular Bid	Third	Coastal
1981	Pleasant Colony	Third	Summing
1987	Alysheba	Fourth	Bet Twice
1989	Sunday Silence	Second	Easy Goer
1997	Silver Charm	Second	Touch Gold
1998	Real Quiet	Second	Victory Gallop
1999	Charismatic	Third	Lemon Drop Kid
2002	War Emblem	Eighth	Sarava
2003	Funny Cide	Third	Empire Maker
2004	Smarty Jones	Second	Birdstone

schedule of three races in five weeks, at longer distances than most have run previously in their careers, is probably the most difficult task any horse will face. Couple that with the fact that the Belmont Stakes is the longest of the three races, at one and a half miles, and you can see why there have been only eleven Triple Crown winners.

I touched on a lesser example of euphoria earlier in the book. In 2004, Todd Pletcher was the leading trainer in money earned. His unsurpassed total earnings of $16.49 million were quite impressive and rightfully earned horseplayers' respect at the betting windows. Pletcher's fans are many, and they have the power to cause odds to become inefficient whenever one of his charges is entered in a race. However, a closer look at his overall winning percentage reveals that his entries only win 21 percent of the time. Yes, his win rate is still quite impressive, but these same fans are passing on many opportunities for value plays elsewhere. The odds on Pletcher's charges will drop while others will become elevated.

Blind Faith

The old notion that a horse coming back after a layoff is an unwise bet exposes the third flaw to the EPH: blind faith in outdated beliefs. Blind faith in outdated beliefs means inefficiencies, thus profit to the handicapper. Evidence shows that horses coming back after a layoff of more than thirty days can provide a very high return on investment when the race is handicapped correctly. Why, then, do so many handicapping systems demand that horses coming back from a thirty-one day or longer layoff be eliminated from consideration rather than letting handicappers think for themselves?

Consistent Winners and Consistent Losers

This is not a flaw with the EPH per se, but the mere fact that consistent winners and losers exist at the track proves that inefficiencies exist. If there are inefficiencies, we can exploit them for profit. Clearly, if we were dealing with an efficient pari-mutuel betting pool, every horseplayer, over time, regardless of skill, could probably break even at the track. Actually, considering the tracks' takeouts, every player would have to lose the same amount. Of course, this is not true. Just look at the professionals, consistently winning money at the races, while other non-professional bettors remain perennial losers. Here is a sure bet: Professional players are constantly seeking new insight into the game. They know that even the simplest of angles may uncover value among inefficiencies in the pool; however, when use of these methods becomes widespread, the inefficiencies disappear.

In summary, these flaws create inefficiencies in the betting pool:

1. Races in which fear, greed, and euphoria are prominent (e.g., last race of the day, provided that it is not the second half of the late double, or major races like the Belmont Stakes).
2. Popular trainers or jockeys.
3. Blind faith in outdated beliefs (e.g., horses with traditionally unfavorable data, such as one coming back after a layoff).

Consistent winners and perennial losers prove beyond a doubt that these flaws create inefficiencies, and inefficiencies create opportunities for profit.

Inefficiencies do not exist in every race. We need to be flexible. We need to have strategies for both efficient and inefficient races. In the second chapter, we will discuss the definition of a "zero-sum" game and the origins of efficient and inefficient betting pools. But, let us first take a quick look at a simple angle of mine that is useful in exploiting the EPH's third flaw, horses with traditionally unfavorable data, more specifically, those coming back after a layoff.

Layoffs

Horses coming back after a layoff between 31 and 120 days are traditionally overlooked by the betting public because the layoff is viewed as an unfavorable situation for a horse to win the race. Insiders (owners and trainers) will therefore do their best to perpetuate the oversight by disguising the current class of the horse as well as their own intentions for their charge.

Two things must be understood before we begin. First, to affect the betting pool significantly and, thus, the odds on the tote board, a relatively large amount of money must be wagered on a horse. We can be reasonably certain that the average two-dollar win bettor does not cause drastic changes in odds. More likely, it is the work of insiders, who, having a great deal of confidence in their entry, have wagered large amounts, causing the odds to descend. This practice is neither illegal nor unethical. They are neither fixing the race nor betting against themselves.

Outsiders are not fortunate enough to know what the insiders know. Therefore, as with trading stocks, we must "follow the money." The tote board can tell us three things about the money flow:

1. The odds in comparison to a horse's last race.
2. The overall trend of the day's odds.
3. The percentage of money the horse has attracted for win, place, and show.

Second, insiders will be taking care not to tip off the betting masses to their intentions. The reason is that an entire crowd of two-dollar bettors could collectively depress the odds of a horse and eat away at the insiders' profits. They prevent this in two ways:

1. In the last race prior to a layoff, trainers will slightly lower a horse in class (including but not limited to claiming horses), then slightly bring him back up in class, at higher odds, subsequent to the layoff. (Horses being raised in class generally do not attract as much attention as those being lowered.) However, for all practical purposes, the trainer is simply returning the horse to its rightful class, so to the untrained eye it only appears that the horse is moving higher. Therefore, our first step is to review the past-performance charts to find horses coming back from a layoff (31 to 120 days without a race) that show the kind of class manipulation I have just described.

2. Insiders (trainers, owners, friends, relatives) will wait patiently to make their bets as close to post time as possible. We should as well.

My research has shown that betting on a horse coming back after a layoff and following the insiders' lead will produce winners slightly more than 20 percent of the time. Therefore, I have placed the minimum acceptable odds for such a horse at 9-1. This gives us a return on investment of 100 percent in a ten-bet series. We are risking $2 x 10 bets or $20 to win two $2 bets at 9-1. Our total return from the two 9-1 winners is $40, or a 100 percent gain on the total amount wagered ($20). Considering that the insiders are, indeed, waiting until the last possible moment to place their bets, we look for horses whose odds lower at least two sequential clicks (i.e., 5-1 to 9-2 to 4-1, or 7-2 to 3-1 to 5-2) in the five minutes before post time. Let us look at an example:

ODDS

HORSE #	P-10 MINUTES	P-5 MINUTES	POST TIME
Horse 1	25-1	10-1	9-1
Horse 2	20-1	10-1	8-1
Horse 3	18-1	12-1	10-1

Only horse #3 qualifies as its odds lowered two sequential clicks (11-1, 10-1) in the five minutes before post. While horse #2 also dropped two sequential clicks (9-1; 8-1), it is below our minimum acceptable odds of 9-1. Horse #1 only dropped one click to 9-1 in the five minutes before post.

Perhaps the strongest indicator of insider confidence is a decidedly higher proportion of money bet to win on a horse rather than to place. If a horse is attracting at least twice the percentage of money bet on it to win than to place, we should be especially interested in it. However, we should not eliminate a horse if it does not meet this criterion. We should use this information to confirm our selection, but at the same time we should consider making a place bet. Here's an example:

POOL	TOTAL	HORSE 1	HORSE 2	HORSE 3	HORSE 4
Win	$20,000	$8,000	$6,000	$4,000	$2,000
Place	$10,000	$4,000	$3,500	$1,000	$1,500

Horse #3 appears to be attracting inside money because it has 20 percent of the win pool, as opposed to only 10 percent of the place pool. There is an inefficiency in the place pool; therefore, we can be assured that the place bet is a better value than a win bet.

In summary, here are our guidelines for playing the Layoff Angle, and exploiting the third flaw in the EPH, blind faith in outdated beliefs.

1. The horse must be coming back from a 31- to a 120-day layoff.
2. It must have been slightly dropped in class the last race prior to the layoff.
3. It must be moving slightly up in class today.
4. It must have current odds of 9-1 or higher (as close to post time as possible).
5. Its odds must lower at least two sequential clicks in the last five minutes before post time.

Remember, a place bet is a better value when there is a disproportionately larger percentage of money bet on a particular horse to win than to place. Wait until the last possible moment to make your bet.

The eighth race at Churchill Downs on November 4, 2004, was an $80,000 optional claimer for three year olds and up. My selection was obvious.

Only three horses (Artemus Sunrise, Founding Chairman, Scat Sam Man) were coming back from a 31- to a 120-day layoff. Founding Chairman's last race was the $100,000 Kentucky

NAME	# DAYS SINCE LAST	CLASS DROP IN LAST ?	CLASS JUMP TODAY?	POST TIME ODDS	ODDS DROP 2 CLICKS?	11/04/04 FINISH
Without a Doubt	20	Yes	Yes	1-1 Fav.		2nd
Ministers Wild Cat	18	Yes	Yes	2-1		4th
Artemus Sunrise	**34**	**Yes**	**Yes**	**11-1**	**Yes**	**1st**
Founding Chairman	40	No	No	11-1		7th
Scat Sam Man	33	No	Yes	9-2		6th
Engineered	18	Yes	Yes	29-1		3rd
Ruba Dub Dub	18	No	No	21-1		5th

Cup Turf Dash, and before that he had raced in an optional claimer for $50,000. He did not qualify under guidelines two and three, so I eliminated him. Scat Sam Man made two successive jumps in class; therefore I eliminated him according to guideline two. This left me watching the odds only on Artemus Sunrise, and as he met the requirements for guideline five, I placed $16 to win and $32 to place on him. The win bet returned $201.60, and the place bet returned $57.60 for a net profit of $211.20.

2

The Psychology of Betting
The Zero-Sum Game

It is important that serious handicappers understand the psychology of betting because it helps us distinguish between efficient and inefficient races. We already know we can profit from inefficiencies, but can we profit from efficiencies in the betting pool? Yes. So, we must develop strategies designed for betting both types of races. To do this, we must understand that people bet on horses for different reasons and that there are different types of gamblers — professional, rational, and irrational. Being aware of these distinctions between players can help a serious handicapper make sense of what is happening on the tote board and use it to his or her advantage. Remember, horse racing is a zero-sum game; no player can win without another losing, and it is important to understand why some players are consistently successful and others are not.

Psychological Profiles of the Players

Three major types of players bet on horses: professional players, rational players, and irrational players. Professional players bet for profit. Rational players bet because the external benefits derived from betting are greater than their losses. Irrational players expect to profit, but for a multitude of reasons their expectations are never realized. In essence, professional players make odds efficient, while both the rational and irrational players undeniably finance the professional players' efforts.

Professionals or highly skilled players profit on average from other players at the track. Cold and calculating, they are anything but irrational. Their winnings cover their life expenses, which may include mortgage or rent payments, income lost by not working a regular job, and the costs incurred to stay proficient and competitive. These professional players profit only to the extent that other less-skilled players are willing to lose money to them at the track. Without the less-skilled players, the professionals cannot survive. Most professionals would view any external benefits they receive (aside from profit) as distractions.

Rational players bet on horses because they obtain some sort of external benefit. Most rational players are aspiring to reach the professional level. Because this realization can be an expensive proposition, knowledge is an extremely valuable external benefit of playing. If they know that they cannot make money from betting, they may simply quit. This is rational behavior because they pay careful attention to their lessons. Rational players are also those who bet just because they enjoy the game or studying how to play. They are willing to play even though they expect to lose. Remember: Horse-race betting becomes a positive-sum game when players gain pleasure or profit from playing. While a single $2 bettor cannot make any impact upon the betting pool, the $2 bettors, en masse, can and do affect the odds. Because irrational and rational players forever cause odds inefficiencies, the value-conscious professionals analyze handicapping information to identify what they consider overlays, or undervalued horses. In turn, they form qualified opinions about a horse's odds such as "this horse should have odds of 2-1 or more." In any case, professional players are better analysts: They are more attentive, they act faster, and they organize handicapping data more effectively and efficiently than do irrational or rational players.

Irrational players fail to accept that they cannot profit from betting on horses. They repeat the same mistakes while expecting different results. Irrational players either refuse to heed past experience or insist upon learning in very costly and inefficient ways.

You should be aware of two other minor types of players: manipulators and allocators. Manipulators decrease pool efficiency by attempting to force odds away from where they should be. They produce and disseminate false information with the sole purpose of either frightening or enticing bettors. They often place small bets on a longshot to create a downward momentum that, in turn, causes the odds on their true selection to rise. The information with which they play is priceless because only the manipulator is aware that he or she has changed the odds. Any major player who relies strictly on the tote board for making a selection is vulnerable to the manipulators' maneuver. Manipulators test the resolve of other players. Contrarian thinking is the best defense against the manipulator.

On the other hand, allocators hedge their bets by making other bets to offset their risk. Allocators can be professional, irrational, or rational. If they are of a conservative nature, the reduced risk exposure may make them feel more comfortable. If they are not averse to risk, offsetting their bets may increase their profitability by reducing losses attributable to unexpected outcomes. Allocators contribute to pool efficiency only to the extent of their skill in making winning selections. That is the reason they can be professional, irrational, or rational. A serious handicapper could certainly be a professional allocator.

It is enough to be aware of the presence of the manipulator, and his or her unethical, but legal, methods. Allocators will be discussed further toward the end of this book because their method offers a valuable money management tool that can help increase our profits. Continuing with our discussion of the major players, we will now examine their preferences.

Major Player Preferences

Irrational players will generally play every race on the card. They are not selective with their bets. Rational players will not play every race on the card. They want to learn to be professionals; knowledge is their most treasured external benefit, but they know it's a high-priced education, and they will be as selective as they can in placing their wagers.

So, what races do major players hone in on? Professional players are able to endure long periods of time between bets and do not go to the track every day. Chances are that when they do, they will only make one well-placed bet. Professionals bide their time waiting for a golden opportunity, and at precisely the right moment they will drop a substantial win wager on a horse.

Now that we've identified the types of players and their preferences, we must turn our attention to how Wall Street principles apply to turning a profit at the betting windows.

If we categorize and compare the different types of horses and stocks, we find that maidens and some claimers, as well as two- and three-year-olds, most closely resemble what Wall Street refers to as penny stocks. As a matter of fact, so do horses coming back after layoffs. Low prices, limited financial information, and an uncertainty about the ability to continue operation are all characteristics of companies that trade as penny stocks. There is also a wide margin of earnings estimates for these enterprises, making predictions concerning the movement of their price very uncertain. It is usually the unsophisticated investor, motivated by greed, who purchases shares of stock in such companies. These investors are like the irrational and rational handicappers. However, skillful traders, willing to accept high risk, can often find their way to above-average returns by allocating some money to penny stocks. The same principle holds true for the professional horseplayer who bets on maidens and some claimers, as well as on two- and three-year-olds. Referring back to what we know about the psychological profiles of the three different types of players, and considering that we will find the number of irrational and rational players betting these horses is far greater than the professionals, one can safely assume that odds inefficiencies will prevail. The amount of money a professional is willing to risk on these particular horses is just not enough to compete with the amount bet by irrational and rational players.

At the other end of the spectrum, we have allowance and handicap runners, horses three years old and up. These animals most closely compare with blue-chip stocks. Higher prices, abundance of financial information, continuous flow of up-to-the-minute press releases, and dividends are typical qualities of a blue-chip company. There is also a narrow margin of earnings estimates for these concerns, making their price movements very predictable. Money managers of large mutual funds and pension plans allocate large sums of money to investing in these companies. These money managers closely resemble professional horseplayers, who will be highly discriminating with their picks but will wager a high amount on the selections once they are confident they have a winner. In spite of the considerable size of the bet, they do not consider it a risky venture. Penny stock investors find that the asking price for blue-chip stocks is too high for their tastes. Simultaneously, a blue-chip stock does not satisfy their psychological need for risk-taking. Irrational and rational handicappers usually have a misguided belief that the odds on these horses are too low to warrant their consideration. Therefore, because most of the betting pool comprises wagers by professionals, we can expect these horses' odds to be efficient.

We can now conclude that both irrational and rational players prefer to take higher risks for greater rewards by wagering on most races on the card. We have found that they drive odds inefficiencies in races where information is unfavorable or scarce and where there is a great deal of uncertainty — races consisting of younger, cheaper, lesser-raced horses. Why do these types of bettors do this? They either refuse to heed past experience or derive some sort of external benefit, other than profit, by doing so. We can expect that the favorites in these races are not accurate predictors of the ultimate winner and, consequently, the percentage for winning favorites will fall below the 33 percent average, which is the norm.

Conversely, professionals prefer to take less risk for reward but will accordingly adjust their wagers to reflect their higher chances of being correct in their selection. They support odds efficiencies by acting faster when analyzing and effectively organizing handicapping data. Professionals will control the betting pool in races that feature older horses with long and successful racing histories. Why do they do this? Very simply, professionals expect to profit from their actions. We can expect that the favorites in these races are somewhat accurate predictors of the eventual winner and that they will be victorious more than 33 percent of the time.

Supporting Our Conclusions

We should all be familiar with the plethora of published mathematical studies that prove that over the long term, favorites will win 33 percent of all races. This is not a guarantee that given a small sample of eighteen races over a two-day period at, say, Saratoga, the favorite will emerge as the winner six times. Indeed, favorites could lose all eighteen of these races and still achieve the expected 33 percent win rate by the end of a given year.

Up until now, we have theorized that certain races, and probably certain tracks that frequently card large quantities of these races, will show either a positive or negative deviation from the 33 percent favorites winning norm. We know that the public influences the market or betting pool, thus correctly or incorrectly selecting the favorite. This is what creates efficient races and inefficient races.

By looking at a large and random sample of races, we can, with great confidence, determine the types of races in which even the most casual bettors are adept at predicting the outcome and races in which they are not. Those at which the public is adept can be considered efficient and those at which the public is not skillful can be called inefficient. Using a random sample of 1,300 races, I recorded the following results:

	TTL SMPL	2-YR OLDS	3-YR OLDS	3-YRS & ^	4-YR OLDS	4-YRS & ^
# Races	1,300	70	250	740	10	230
# Win Fav	410	10	50	230	10	110
Win %	31.5	14.3	20	31.1	100	47.8

If we disregard the rather large anomaly recorded for the four-year-olds, it is still apparent that the public fares much better when predicting the winner of races for older horses than it does for their younger counterparts. The favorites in races for two- and three-year-olds won only 14.3 percent and 20 percent, respectively, of the time. Favorites in races for three-year-olds and up had a win rate just under the expected 31.5 percent for this sample, while in races for four-year-olds and up, favorites enjoyed a win rate of 47.8 percent.

	TTL SMPL	SPRINT	ROUTE	MAID	CLAIM	ALLOW	H'CAP
# Races	1,300	710	590	430	560	260	50
# Wn Fv	410	210	200	116	176	97	21
Win %	31.5	29.6	33.9	27	31.4	37.3	42

Here, low-purse races (maidens, claimers), with relatively inexperienced runners had a significantly lower percentage of winning favorites than did high-purse races (handicaps) with

experienced entries. It is definitely worth noting the 29.6 percent win rate for sprinting favorites, in contrast to the 33.9 percent win rate for horses running a route. It is my belief that the
longer race allows a horse and his jockey to correct any early
mistakes before the end of the race, while races under a mile
are less forgiving. While not shown above, there was virtually
no difference between the winning percentages of favorite fillies and mares and favorite colts and geldings. The sharp eye
will undoubtedly notice that the race type that has the highest
probability of a winning favorite, thus the easiest to predict, is
the handicap for four-year-olds and up run at a distance of a
mile or longer.

The very fact that you are reading this manual means that
you are a rational horseplayer. The question that remains is
this: Are you a professional as well? The answer depends on
your personal risk tolerance and your goals. In the next chapter you will find nine questions designed to create your own
personal risk profile. Upon completion, you will be better able
to decide what type of betting strategy is right for you.

Personal Risk Profile
The Best Strategy for You

It is very important for the professional handicapper to have a betting strategy that he or she adheres to with great conviction. Because I do not have the luxury of sitting down with each and every reader of this book, I have prepared a list of questions for you to determine your unique risk profile, thus the best betting strategy for you.

First, though, let's talk about risk. The first step in managing gambling risk is to understand it. Most people imagine risk as a negative. The word evokes thoughts of parachuting, breaking the law, or going on a blind date. In the context of gambling, people associate risk with betting on a longshot.

Fear of losing money is one reason that horseplayers choose conservative betting strategies like playing the favorite. Greed often drives handicappers to more aggressive play such as wagering on longshots. The category to which people are suited depends largely on their life circumstances. How old are they? Are they married? Do they have children? How much have they saved? What is their income? How much debt do they have?

The key is to match strategies to goals. Is the goal to preserve the bankroll, increase its size, or generate an income to cover household expenses? What is the deadline for reaching these goals?

Your answers to these questions will enable you to find the right balance between the risk you are willing to take and the return you hope to achieve. For example, handicappers pursuing a long-term goal, such as buying a second home, will be most concerned with the long-term growth of their bankroll and may opt for a more conservative betting strategy.

Answer the following questions in order to determine which method is best for your particular profile. Remember: Be honest. The answers you give are very important in determining whether you will have the discipline to be successful with a particular course of action. You will not be successful using a strategy with which you are not psychologically comfortable.

The Questions

1. If higher returns on my wagers were needed to meet my goals, I would:
   a. Feel comfortable with bets that might occasionally lose during a given month.
   b. Feel comfortable with bets that might frequently lose during a given month as long as my average return is higher over time.
   c. Not feel comfortable with bets that frequently lose during a given month.
2. If my bankroll dropped in value by 10 percent while other horseplayers enjoyed their wins, I would most likely be inclined to:
   a. Switch to another strategy or quit playing horses all together.
   b. Consider increasing the amount I bet.
   c. Stay the course.
3. If I were offered a choice among one of two scratch-off lottery tickets (one worth $1 and the other worth $400), $200 in cash, or a combination of half the cash and half the amount of one of the lottery tickets (the value of which is unkonw at the time of the coie, I would mostly likely take:
   a. A one-in-two chance of receiving $400 if I could guess which ticket was the $400 winner.

   b. Half the $200 in cash ($100) and half of whatever my chosen lottery ticket paid (50 cents or $200).

   c. The $200 in cash.

4. When I consider my overall situation, my most important objective is to:

   a. Increase my bankroll over time.

   b. Preserve my bankroll.

   c. Use some winnings for household expenses, including entertainment, and increase my bankroll at a lesser rate over time.

5. If my bankroll were $2,000 today, and I wanted to meet an important goal two years from now, I would feel most comfortable with a strategy that had me betting:

   a. Only on favorites.

   b. On favorites and longshots.

   c. Only on longshots.

6. When it comes to wagering, I am most comfortable with horses that:

   a. Have odds of 1-9.

   b. Have odds of 1-1.

   c. Have odds of 9-1.

7. I am offered a chance to buy into a business venture for a $2,000 investment, and I have twenty-four hours to think about it. The venture has a 50 percent chance of paying back $10,000 within five years and a 50 percent chance of losing my entire investment. If I had the $2,000 available to invest, I would:

   a. Pass; it is too risky.

   b. Jump in with both feet; the upside far outweighs the downside.

   c. Carefully think about it, even if it means missing the deadline.

8. Consider the range of high and low possibilities that

might result from a $2,000 bankroll in three different scenarios over a one-year period. Keep in mind that wagers offering higher returns involve more risk. Which range of possible outcomes would be most acceptable to you?

    a. Best case: $2,550; worst case: $1,725.

    b. Best case: $3,082; worst case: $1,459.

    c. Best case: $4,177; worst case: $912.

9. How long will it be before you will want to draw money (other than for gambling expenses) from your bankroll?

    a. Today. I want to go out to eat, and I should buy gas first.

    b. Next month. The mortgage is due.

    c. Two summers from now. I have my eye on a new boat, and I want to pay cash.

Now use the following key to compute your score.

1. A - 2 points
   B - 1 point
   C - 3 points
	4. A - 1 point
	   B - 3 points
	   C - 2 points
		7. A - 3 points
		   B - 1 point
		   C - 2 points

2. A - 3 points
   B - 1 point
   C - 2 points
	5. A - 3 points
	   B - 2 points
	   C - 1 point
		8. A - 3 points
		   B - 2 points
		   C - 1 point

3. A - 1 point
   B - 2 points
   C - 3 points
	6. A - 3 points
	   B - 2 points
	   C - 1 point
		9. A - 3 points
		   B - 2 points
		   C - 1 point

(9 to 14 points) You are an aggressive bettor and should feel comfortable using a method designed for longshots the preponderance of the time. You must be prepared to weather short-term fluctuations. The types of races that are best for an aggressive system are maiden, claiming, and those restricted to two- and three-year-olds. Sprint races are conducive to your style of play.

(15 to 21 points) As a moderate, you need the best of both

worlds: longshots and favorites. You must be flexible. This requires the discipline to conform, without fail, to each distinct style of play. You must master playing longshots and favorites and stay true to their course, even if one is outperforming the other. Do not give up on one method because doing so could ultimately lead to overall losses as the other may fail. Short-term fluctuations with either approach are to be expected.

(22 to 27 points) You are a conservative player and should feel at home using a system designed for favorites most of the time. You must be prepared to accept a return less than that of the aggressive player. Allowance and handicap races offer the best chance for a player like you, provided they are restricted to older horses, three years old and up. Also, remember the favorite wins more than its share of route races.

Remember, too, that each handicapper has unique goals and tolerance for risk. Once a plan is chosen, it is wise to stick with it for the short to intermediate term (up to a year). Give your plan a chance to work. That being said, it is also prudent to re-evaluate your personal situation and tolerance for risk at least once a year. People's financial goals change when they get married, have a baby, retire, etc. After a year with an aggressive strategy, you may find that your tolerance for risk is not as high as you thought. You may not enjoy yourself because you get physically ill with each start of a race. Answer these survey questions again. Likewise, after a year, if you find that you are getting bored, deviating from your conservative plan by making wild action bets, answer these questions again. Your job is to be as honest as possible.

Strategies for Aggressive Selections

While aggressive selections, or longshot plays, do not offer as high a winning percentage as conservative selections, or favorite plays, they offer the professional player a chance at a fantastic return on each dollar wagered. Our primary focus here will be to identify the types of races in which the average two-dollar bettor generally fails to select the favorite. Remember that when this happens, both favorites and longer shots will be inefficiently priced, but only the longer shots will be overlays, or value plays.

Longshot or Higher-Risk Play

I mentioned in chapter one that investors would not invest in a high-risk stock unless it offered a higher return on investment than one considered less risky. Similarly, a professional handicapper would not bet on a high-odds horse unless he or she was convinced it was a solid overlay, or value play. In chapter two I said that a skillful stock trader, willing to accept high risk, could often reap above-average returns by investing in penny stocks. The same principle applies to handicappers. Because betting on maiden claimers closely resembles investing in penny stocks, it is logical to think that a professional handicapper who is willing to accept high risk also could win big by betting on maiden claimers from time to time. Maiden claimers are aggressive plays and are certainly worthy of a strategy all their own.

Maiden Claimers Entered in a Sprint

One of the toughest tests a handicapper faces is the maiden claiming race. Just by looking at the pure definition of the race (non-winners), we can see that we are dealing with a very sorry group of older horses. Plainly, they usually lack any acceptable measure of class, condition, or speed. Their past performances are either riddled with unfavorable data or are limited in scope.

Those handicappers who are averse to risk should, if possible, avoid these races. However, depending on the track they frequent, some players just do not have that luxury, unless they are comfortable betting races via simulcast or the Internet. So, both the risk avoider and the risk taker would do well to understand them.

A few years ago I was giving handicapping tips to a player who frequents Canterbury Park, a track that cards many of these types of races, and he asked how I identify possible contenders in maiden races. To that end, I would like to share with you what I believe are the five major considerations regarding maidens: age, workouts, trainers, tote board, and pedigree.

First, I begin by eliminating maidens four years old and up. I view them as chronic losers. You will not find any better selection at the track than the lightly raced three-year-old pitted against a group of unsuccessful older horses. Second, I eliminate horses that are not true three-year-olds, meaning I stick with three-year-olds foaled in January, February, or March. Although a horse officially becomes a yearling on the New Year's day following its birth, a horse foaled in May or June is not as developed as one foaled earlier in the year. What I do is eliminate every four-year-old and up and those three-year-olds foaled in May throughout the remainder of the year. This leaves us with betting choices consisting solely of three-year-olds either with or without recent past performances to analyze. For now, we will look at three-year-olds with no races and only workouts.

My preferred method for analyzing workouts for unraced horses evolved from the premise that the length and frequency of workouts are just as important as, if not more important than, the speed. The reason the speed factor needs to be discounted is that many variables can affect a horse's time. A few that immediately come to mind are weight, time of day, and running path. I do not believe that even the clockers are aware of exactly how much weight a horse is carrying via the exercise rider, lead weights, etc., during a morning workout. Although some jockeys work horses, usually an exercise rider who weighs considerably more than a jockey works the horse. In such a case, the times would be slower. If a horse is working out early on a clean and fresh track, the workout is going to be relatively faster than a later workout over a disturbed track. Finally, while clockers know the running path of the horse in question, whether it hugged the rail or saved ground, this information is not disseminated to the public.

The distance of a workout goes a long way in disclosing a horse's readiness and a trainer's intention. For horses preparing for a sprint race, workouts of three furlongs are extremely commonplace and offer the bettor nothing significant so should be disregarded whether or not a bullet is posted. A work of four furlongs is fine, but a work of five or six usually indicates the trainer is ready to run the horse. We will not discuss route races because we are confining all of our aggressive plays to sprints, as we already know they offer a better chance than routes at collecting higher payoffs at the betting window. If at all possible, we do not want to negate our efforts.

Workouts are not arbitrary things. Once a training program begins, workouts should be performed at regular intervals. This helps handicappers determine whether a horse is in peak condition. Here are my suggested rules for evaluating and eliminating horses only showing workouts:

Sprints 6 to 7 1/2 Furlongs

1. Only one workout: It must have been a bullet in the past ten days, at five furlongs or longer. If the horse does not show this pattern in its workout line, eliminate it.

2. Two workouts: Both must have been in the past seventeen days, with one at least five furlongs and one at least four furlongs. One of them must have been a bullet. If the horse does not show this pattern in its workout line, eliminate it.

3. Three or more workouts: Three must have been in the past thirty-eight days, with one at least five furlongs and one at least four furlongs. One of them must have been a bullet. If the horse does not show this pattern in its workout line, eliminate it.

4. No workouts in the past thirty-eight days: Eliminate the horse from contention.

For sprints at five furlongs or less, subtract one furlong from the distance requirements.

We require a bullet because the horse should be in good enough condition to produce it, and the trainer should want to use the workout to simulate an actual race as closely as possible.

After having eliminated these maidens based upon workouts, we should look next to trainer patterns.

To its credit, the *Daily Racing Form* provides handicappers with a lot of useful statistics on trainers, such as how they fare with a first-time starter, second-time starter, in maiden claiming races, switching from a maiden special weight to a maiden claiming, first-time using blinkers, blinkers on and blinkers off, first time on Lasix, after layoffs, on dirt and turf, etc. But in my opinion, a player needs to take the process a step or two further in order to see what others cannot.

You could easily construct a spreadsheet with trainers'

names written vertically down one side and, again, take the basic categories the DRF offers a few steps further. For instance, you might construct a spreadsheet that looks like this:

TRAINER NAME	3RD TIME START	4TH TIME START	2ND TIME BLINKERS	3RD TIME BLINKERS	2ND TIME LASIX	3RD TIME LASIX

Keeping these detailed records for every trainer even at one track requires a heck of a lot of work. I chose to mention it in this section about trainers, not to use as an elimination tool, but more to bring to light that every now and then you will discover an aberration that might make you a boatload of money. You may discover that Terri Trainer at Lemon Grove Park wins with 50 percent of her charges when they are running for the third time on Lasix. The betting public may read her abysmal record and ignore her entry, and you find her horse at odds of 37-1. That's when you go for the jugular. Enough said.

Now, I am sure that I will get some argument here, but I actually prefer that maidens showing races in their past performances actually ran *third* or worse their last time out. My reasoning is twofold: First, a second-place finish tells me that the trainer was trying to win with the horse but failed. Second, when playing maidens, we are looking for high odds, and we are far more likely to find them with horses that the public generally overlooks. Remember, we must get comfortable with contrarian thinking.

Referring back to the tote-board segment of our angle for horses coming back after a layoff (see chapter one), pay close attention to horses whose odds lower at least two sequential clicks in the five minutes before post time. However, I chose to exclude the 9-1 minimum odds requirement because considering we have a race consisting of similar horses, there is a good chance that minimum requirement will not be met. However, in a race where there is only one horse with unfavorable data, such as one coming back after a layoff or one that finished out of the money last time out, it is more likely that its odds will be elevated to 9-1 or higher.

Finally, do not give too much attention to the pedigree of maidens. When any trainer is given a top-dollar horse, purchased at $100,000 or more, he or she will prefer to race the horse into condition as opposed to working it hard in anticipation of its first race. No trainer will risk injuring a top-dollar horse before it even gets to the gate. Also, except for first-time starters, the horses entered at this level are usually of such poor quality that pedigree does not mean much.

In summary, these are the most important factors aggressive players should consider when playing maidens entered in a sprint:

1. **RACE:** Only play on sprints for maidens.
2. **AGE:** Only play on true three-year-olds.
3. **WORKOUTS:** Consider workouts only in the absence of any races in the past performance lines. See rules outlined above.
4. **TRAINERS:** Stay away from horses whose trainer obviously tried to win the last time out but missed. Include any horse that finished *third* or worse the last time out. Think about keeping your own records on trainer patterns.
5. **TOTE BOARD:** Look at horses whose odds lower at least two sequential clicks in the last five minutes before post time.

6. **PEDIGREE:** Remember that a top-dollar horse is not necessarily ready to win the first or second time out. Pedigree means nothing at this stage of the game.

7. The bet (for win bettors) is on the horse with the best finish last time out (third, fourth, fifth, etc.) (Remember, we have already excluded first- and second-place finishers.)

8. In case of ties, the bet is on the horse with the highest posttime odds.

Here's an example from Churchill Downs on November 4, 2004. Race six was a maiden claiming for Thoroughbreds three years old and up. This six and one-half-furlong sprint was run over the dirt and attracted fourteen starters.

NAME	AGE	MNTH FOALED	LAST FINISH	POST TIME ODDS	11/04/04 FINISH
Lady Laabity	4	March	None	106-1	8th
Rainbow Wrangler	3	March	11th	136-1	6th
American Power	3	May	11th	3-1	5th
Not On My Watch	3	May	2nd	2-1 Favorite	7th
Brents Burner	4	April	None	46-1	9th
Arrive	3	February	5th	30-1	10th
Union Square	3	February	4th	7-2	3rd
Halo Hallo	3	February	None	14-1	11th
Sam's Bad Boy	3	April	Lst Distanced	86-1	12th
Wild in the Lane	4	April	5th	18-1	13th
Jimmy One Punch	**3**	**February**	**3rd**	**8-1**	**1st**
Smoken Rollin	4	February	4th	17-1	2nd
Traded	3	April	9th	37-1	14th
One Eyed Gambler	3	March	2nd	23-1	4th

Upon completing the first two steps, Rainbow Wrangler, Arrive, Union Square, Halo Hallo, Jimmy One Punch, and One Eyed Gambler remained. Halo Hallo only showed workouts and did not meet the requirements, so I eliminated him. I also eliminated One Eyed Gambler because he placed second in his last race. Left with Rainbow Wrangler, Arrive, Union Square, and Jimmy One Punch, I placed an eleven-dollar win bet on Jimmy One Punch for he had the best finish (third) last time out.

Horse	Win	Place	Show
Jimmy One Punch	$19.80	$9.60	$5.60
Smoken Rollin		$15.20	$8.40
Union Square			$4.00

Note in the previous chapter that the public made Not On My Watch the 2-1 favorite most likely because of his second-place finish last time out. He finished seventh!

For the less aggressive player, this selection method also works very well with place and show bets. Between November 1, 2004, and November 10, 2004, a two-dollar place bet coupled with a four-dollar show bet returned $170.60 over nineteen different races. With a total outlay of only $114, it had a return on investment of 49.6 percent!

This was our second method, or angle, for aggressive bettors. The first one was for horses coming back after a layoff. Some of the principles outlined here can be interchanged with other longshot systems. Remember that our winning percentage will not be as high with these methods as it is with angles for conservative, favorite play, and it must be reflected in your money management. When we are through discussing the systems for both styles of play, I will show you strategies for managing your money.

Claiming Races for Non-Winners of Two Races Lifetime

Claiming races make up more than 65 percent of all race cards, yet they are probably the least understood by bettors. They have been called the great equalizer, but do not confuse this with the ability to drive efficient odds, because, as I discussed earlier, claiming races are less than efficient. Competition from novice owners is promoted by permitting them to enter the Sport of Kings at an economical cost. In addition, if a horse is entered in a five thousand-dollar claiming race, any owner or trainer can claim it for that price.

One of the greatest myths surrounding the claiming race is that a horse moving down in class is tantamount to an automatic win for the owner and trainer. This is not true. A chronic loser in a higher class becomes used to losing and will most likely continue to lose in a lower class. While a *slight* drop in class could mean an attempt at winning the purse, a *large* drop most likely signifies that the horse is no longer competitive and the horse's connections are simply trying to unload it. They would never want to risk losing a good horse by having it claimed out from under them.

However, we know from examining how trainers place their horses after a layoff that they may try to mask their intentions by slight adjustments in class. Borrowing from that angle, we will once again look at the horse's prior race.

When we looked at maiden claiming races, we stated that there is not any better selection at the track than the lightly raced three-year-old battling a gathering of unsuccessful older horses. However, in a claiming race for non-winners of two races, three-year-olds are usually outclassed. Once again, trainers prefer to race a horse until they find the level that best suits their charge. Why? Risk is involved in running a three-year-old in a claiming race for non-winners of two races lifetime because the horse could be claimed at a bargain. Therefore, for purposes of this angle, we will eliminate any three-year-olds from our list of contenders.

In keeping with our search for high-odds horses, we eliminate any horse that finished first in his last effort. This means we are eliminating horses that broke their maiden in their last race, no great feat considering the quality of competition at that level. Furthermore, unless a horse is moving slightly high-

er in class, a second-place finish could again indicates the trainer was trying to win but failed. Trying and failing indicate the
horse is simply outclassed at the current level.

Therefore, our guidelines look like this.

1. Eliminate any horse less than four years of age.
2. Eliminate any horse that finished first its last time out.
   Also, *unless* it is moving slightly higher in class, eliminate
   any horse that finished second in its last effort.
3. Watch for horses being strategically maneuvered between
   classes.
4. The bet (for win bettors) is on the horse being maneuvered according to our layoff angle.
5. In cases where two or more horses have been maneuvered (a drop in class before today's jump), the bet (for
   win bettors) is on the horse with the best finish (third,
   fourth, fifth, etc.) in its last race. (Remember we have
   already eliminated horses finishing first place and maybe
   second according to the second guideline above.)
6. In races void of maneuvered horses, the bet (for win bettors) is still on the horse with the best finish in its last race.

The second race at Finger Lakes on November 4, 2004, was
for fillies and mares three years old and up that had never won
two races. The claiming price for this event was four thousand
dollars.

NAME	AGE	LAST FINISH	LAST CLASS LEVEL	11/04/04 FINISH
Distinctive Deed	4	5th	Clm 4000 N2L	6th
Hourglass Figure	4	7th	Alw 14900 N2L	Scratched
Its a Jet	**4**	**3rd**	**Clm 4000 N2L**	**1st**
Galloping to Tea	3	6th	Clm 4000 N2L	2nd
Takethemoneyhoney	3	1st	Md 4000	7th
Gotta Lotta Speed	3	5th	Clm 4000 N2L	5th
Bingo Caller	3	4th	Clm 4000 N2L	3rd
Glowing Brite	3	9th	Clm 4000 N2L	4th

I had a very easy job, considering only Distinctive Deed and Its a Jet remained after the initial age elimination. Had Hourglass Figure not scratched, she would have been eliminated because of the very large drop in class. Likewise, if Takethemoneyhoney were a four-year-old, she would have been eliminated because of her first-place finish in a maiden event. Neither of my contenders showed evidence of class manipulation by their respective trainers; therefore, I bet thirty-eight dollars to win on Its a Jet. Why? Her third-place finish in the last race was better than Distinctive Deed's fifth-place finish. Unfortunately, my minimal risk in this race was reflected with a minimal return of $100.70.

Once again, you can see how certain criteria for betting different types of races can be interchanged. Undoubtedly, we will occasionally see our choice edged out at the wire. Do not worry. This is to be expected. You have probably noticed that the phrase "for win bettors" keeps appearing in parentheses. The reason is to keep these angles as simple as possible, but by the time we are finished, you may decide to play these selections in a different manner.

First Time Starters in
Maiden Special Weight Sprints

Again, referring back to chapter two, limited financial information and a wide margin of earnings estimates (meaning that a company's earnings are inconsistent and unpredictable) are characteristics of a penny stock. An investor may buy the "story" of the company, such as a promising new drug or a new type of football league, or a former engineer from one of the big three automakers striking out on his own. These gambles rarely pay off, but when they do, they provide an incredible return on investment. Like maiden claimers, maiden special weights closely resemble penny stocks. Further, maiden special weights, again like maiden claimers, offer the sophisticated handicapper a unique opportunity to make an aggressive play for a huge payoff at the betting window.

However, maiden special weight races are different from the maiden claimers in that they usually have more horses that have never raced. With no visible data other than workouts, the horses entered in these races can contribute to a highly inefficient betting pool at times and simultaneously offer the potential for high rewards. Since this is an aggressive play, I certainly want to look where I can find the most inefficiently priced animals, and that has to be with the horses that have never raced.

Start by eliminating any maiden special weight entrant that has raced.

After that, I believe the three major subjects worthy of discussion regarding maiden special weights are pedigree, workouts, and tote board.

PEDIGREE: There is a certain degree of argument concerning the treatment of pedigree when playing maiden special weights. Some players favor a thorough analysis of bloodlines, targeting two-year-olds sired by a stallion that has a successful record in producing first-time winners. I simply view pedigree as a non-issue. As I said regarding maiden claimers, a top-dollar horse is not necessarily ready to win his first or second time out. I will not eliminate one from contention, but I always keep in mind that a trainer may be simply racing his charge into condition instead of risking injury to the horse via workouts prior to its first race. Obviously, a horse is just as likely to be injured in a race, or even more likely, but try telling that to the owner who has dreamed of watching her horse run a race and has invited her friends and family along for the fun.

WORKOUTS: No one will argue that workouts are extremely important when handicapping a maiden claimer. The two most important factors in selecting a winning first-time starter are workouts and the tote board. To avoid being redundant, I refer you back to the rules outlined above for workouts for maiden claimers. Since we are only considering two selection factors for first-time starters, I suggest that you stringently apply the workout rules.

At this point, you may find you have absolutely no contenders left. That's fine. We pass the race. Go grab a soda.

TOTE BOARD: Regardless of its odds, the horse might be the consensus third choice; the ultimate selection is on the horse that has a proportionately higher amount bet on him to win than to place. Why? Again, this indicates that insiders have a great deal of confidence that their horse is going to come out on top. We already know that the place pool is inefficient relative to the win pool for this horse, so, again, a decision will have to be made whether to bet this horse to win or to place. With this choice, the better wager would be a place bet that is larger than the prescribed win bet.

Let's take a look at the tenth race at Philadelphia Park on November 1, 2004. Twelve horses went in this six-furlong maiden special weights, but only three of them had never raced. I eliminated the other nine.

NAME	LAST WORK	2ND LAST WORK	3RD LAST WORK	BULLETS	11/01/04 FINISH
American Jet	10/26 5F	10/18 5F	09/22 4F	Yes	12th
Caromon	**10/26 5F**	**10/18 5F**	**10/09 5F**	**Yes**	**1st**
Quoit a Journey	10/18 4F	10/05 4F	09/07 3F	Yes	4th

I eliminated American Jet because while he had three or more workouts, his third-to-last was forty days ago, and we require all three to be in the last thirty-eight days. Likewise, Quoit a Journey had three or more workouts, but his third-to-last was fifty-five days ago. In addition, none of Quoit's workouts were at five furlongs, and we require at least one. While the percentage difference between the win and place pools was not as great as I would have liked, I made a judgment call and wagered twenty-eight dollars to place on Caromon. Winning at 6-1 odds, he returned $95.20 for my place bet.

We have limited our last three aggressive angles to sprints because we know they offer a better chance at a winning long-shot than route races. Our first angle for layoffs can be applied to both sprints and routes as we are dealing with a specific horse, not a race. It is my belief that longer races allow a horse and his jockey to correct any early mistakes before the end of the race, while races under a mile are less forgiving. But, is there a generic handicapping method for sprints?

Sprints

Most horseplayers opine that route races are more difficult to handicap than sprints. I hold a dissenting view. If the major-ity were correct, then we would not see such a disparity between the percentages of winning favorites for each type of race. In fact, one would expect to see the percentage of winning favorites for sprint races higher than that for routes. This is not the case.

A little more than 70 percent of all races are sprints. A sprint race is less than one mile and not more than one turn. Most sprints are run at 6 furlongs but may be as long as seven and a half furlongs.

Conventional wisdom holds that a fast breaker, a horse that can set a rapid pace for the first quarter-mile and take the lead while saving ground on the rail, has a distinct advantage over the competition. But what happens when a race is riddled with fast breakers as it most often is? The early leaders will thwart each other's effort and begin to back up in the final stretch. They will also create traffic problems for themselves and quick-ly run out of real estate to correct the mistake.

Well, what if our sprinter lags behind the rest of the pack?

This presents a more severe problem in that a horse that has neither been close to the leaders nor hugged the rail will not have sufficient energy to pass the others during the stretch run. Even if the horse is able to save ground on the rail, he will run into traffic problems, too, as the leaders refuse to open a hole for him. The aforementioned "traffic problems" can be readily seen in the chart comments as "blocked," "bumped," "checked," and "forced wide."

However, the real test of a sprinter's mettle is, indeed, in the last quarter-mile stretch run. It is very important, though, that he runs effectively up until that point. He must stalk, and not lag behind, the leaders from the very start and never for a moment fall out of contention.

Look at each past performance line where the horse ran six furlongs. First, eliminate any horse that was ever more than four lengths off the pace at the half-mile call for any of his past three six-furlong races. This rids us of the closer. Second, eliminate any horse that was in the lead for the first quarter-mile but lost it at the half, for his last three six-furlong races. This rids us of the speedball and dueler, both of whose running styles are subject to almost the same problems as those of the closer. Last, eliminate any horse that has not finished first or second at six furlongs.

Using the horse's best finish (either first or second) at six furlongs, compute the final quarter-mile time for each of the remaining horses. If the horse was leading at the half as well, this is relatively simple. Convert the final time into seconds, subtract the half-mile time, and you have the final quarter-mile time. In races where the horse did not lead at the half, add one-fifth second for each length the horse was off the pace to the actual half-mile time and you will have that horse's half-mile time. The play is on the horse with the fastest final quarter-mile time.

Delaware Park's eighth race on November 1, 2004, was a fantastic example of this angle's effectiveness. Eight horses were entered in this six-furlong allowance, but only three managed to qualify as far as computing the final quarter-mile time.

NAME	FIN. 1/4 MI. TIME	POST TIME ODDS	11/01/04 FINISH
Gotta Rush	:26	7-2	1st
Trickle of Gold	:25 3/5	Scratched	Scratched
Carly'ssilvercharm	:26 2/5	5-2	2nd

For example: In Trickle of Gold's last six-furlong race she ran :22 1/5, :45 3/5, :58 1/5, and 1:11 1/5.

As it happened, she led at the half and won the race. Converting 1:11 1/5 to :71 1/5 and subtracting :45 3/5 we have a final quarter-mile time of :25 3/5.

Trickle of Gold had set the best final quarter-mile time, but she scratched. Carly'ssilvercharm got caught up in a duel through the half (which we do not want to see) and was caught in the stretch by Gotta Rush. Missile Bay, a horse I eliminated because she had never raced at six furlongs, came late to finish third as the 9-5 favorite. My $10 exacta box returned $187 for a net profit of $167.

Remember, most of these races are won by horses that are able to stalk the leaders but do not make their big move until the final two furlongs of the race. This racing style will effectively keep them out of traffic, while allowing them to save ground for solid stretch runs past the tiring pack. This fifth and final angle for the aggressive player will yield a good return because it is yet another example of contrarian thinking.

The overriding strategy with these aggressive methods is to recognize first that the public is usually wrong in its selection of favorites for these types of races. Second, we need to realize what kind of information the public views as favorable to a horse's chances, such as in-the-money finishes last time out. Finally, we must be brave enough to take the road less traveled, think outside the box, and place wagers where others normally would not.

5

Strategies for Conservative Selections

Making conservative selections is far simpler than playing aggressive angles. Payoffs for these conservative selections are obviously going to be lower, but overall this strategy will produce a much higher win percentage than the aggressive longshot angles and if bet with a sound money management system will produce substantial returns over time.

When it comes to applying a conservative strategy to handicapping, the stock market provides a good comparison. Conservative investors, like conservative bettors, want to know where their money is going. They are much more likely to put money into blue-chip stocks with their lengthy histories, ability to generate a profit over time, and the availability of updated information. Similarly, conservative bettors are much better off focusing on allowance and handicap runners, as well as on horses three years old and up, competing in longer races. These horses usually are proven, high-quality contenders with solid histories that Turf writers follow. They are usually predictable when they run a longer race, where trouble can be overcome. Professional handicappers averse to risk know they won't make a killing betting these horses, but over time will realize a profit if they follow these horses closely and choose their spots carefully.

Favorite Play

One angle of conservative betting is targeting the favorite. The purpose here is to spot, within a group of races we already know has a higher-than-average percentage of winning favorites, the favorites that elevate that percentage. We are looking for the crème de la crème.

Follow the Money

In chapter two I showed you that in my random sample of 1,300 races, favorites running in allowance, handicap, and route races win more often than in other types of races. We also know that the big-money professionals will gravitate toward these types of races, thus driving odds efficiencies. So, the astute handicapper, having read this book, should realize that "piggybacking" the big-money professionals' choice to win is a strong percentage play even though he or she may not be getting it at a bargain basement price. Big-money professionals will only bet as long as they are reasonably certain they can collect on these small profit margin plays.

Conversely, the average two-dollar bettor will pass on favorites entered at these levels, reasoning that the small profit margin is not worth the investment and opting instead to bet on a longshot. Their greater satisfaction with a losing wager on a longshot defies logic. This irrational player will freely acknowledge the favorite as the best selection but will leave it to the professionals to bet. Oh, well. Remember that professionals make money from the irrational players' mistakes. The two-dollar bettor's depressing the odds on longer shot horses prevents the favorite (in allowance, handicap, and route races) from becoming an underlay.

Our mission is to pinpoint the exact spot where the favorite is a virtual lock. These spot plays are not as prevalent as the longshot plays of our aggressive angles but, nevertheless, are well worth our time and money.

Our first conservative approach to favorites is similar to the aggressive methods in that we need to determine first what the average two-dollar bettor considers favorable information for a racehorse. Then, we look for horses absent of this information, that, in our estimation, should not be favorites at all but nevertheless are. This occurrence indicates that something is afoot.

The smart money players have stepped in, ignored the obvious favorite, and bet elsewhere. When this situation occurs, I will not go against the collective judgment of big-money professionals, no matter what my personal preferences may be.

Many selection systems teach bettors to hone in on horses that finished in the money last time out, making this what most handicappers consider favorable information. Furthermore, these selection systems hold second-place finishers in higher regard than first-place finishers. In fact, the general betting public likes these second-place finishers so much they tend to overplay them, creating some low level of inefficiency in their odds.

Many bettors discard an allowance horse that finished out of the money and more than five lengths off the winner in its previous races although, as it turns out, those horses do as well as horses with a first-place finish. If we know that horses with a second-place finish last time out are popular among the betting public, then what does it mean when a horse without that honor is sent off as the favorite? It means the big-money professionals have swooped in and are in control of the betting pool. If we follow the money, like we should, our choice has to be the favorite without the second-place finish last time out. It is as simple as that.

In summary, we find our conservative spot plays using the following rules:

1. Only allowance races and handicap races run at a mile or more are playable. Remember that we have this rule because favorites running in allowance, handicap, and route races win more often than in other types of races.
2. Obviously, the play is on the favorite.
3. Pass the race entirely if the favorite finished second his last time out. (Remember that we are looking for horses that are favorites but do not exhibit what the average two dollar bettor considers favorable information.)

On November 5, 2004, the third race at Hawthorne satisfied

all three of the above rules. It was a one and one-eighth mile allowance race for three-year-olds and up.

NAME	LAST FINISH	M/L ODDS	POST TIME ODDS	11/05/04 FINISH
Marion's Man	2nd	3-1	4-1	2nd
Stormin Gen. Tommy	3rd	7-2	7-2	7th
Devil's Diary	1st	4-1	6-1	8th
Subsequently	**3rd**	**6-1**	**3-2 Favorite**	**1st**
Beautiful Angel	6th	8-1	9-1	4th
Chasing the Ghosts	8th	10-1	15-1	9th
All Academic	4th	15-1	24-1	3rd
Settler	7th	15-1	28-1	5th
No Nice	5th	20-1	26-1	10th
One Objective	5th	20-1	84-1	6th

Note that Marion's Man was the morning line favorite at 3-1, most likely due to his second-place finish last time out. When I followed the substantial amount of money being bet on Subsequently, my choice became clear. Subsequently's odds were pummeled and lowered from 6-1 to 3-2 despite his third-place finish last time out. I bet forty dollars to win on this favorite and my investment returned one hundred dollars even.

You may want to experiment with variations of this angle. Try sampling how the *Daily Racing Form* consensus picks perform against other horses that are sent off as the favorite. Look at anything that might really draw the public's attention, such as a popular rider at a certain track, for example Pat Day at Churchill or Keeneland. If the horse he is riding is not sent off as the favorite, there is most likely a very good reason.

Scratches

One of the most legendary rivalries in the history of sports was that of Alydar and Affirmed. In the 1978 Kentucky Derby, Alydar went off as the 6-5 favorite with Affirmed at 9-5. What would Alydar's odds have been had Affirmed scratched that day? Would Affirmed have been less than even money had

Alydar scratched? A horse's chances of winning, and thus the conservative professional's, are greatly improved by the elimination of obvious competition. The co-favorite will not become a huge underlay; it deserves to attract more money because its chances have been markedly improved.

It is said that the morning line has little or no value in handicapping and, for the most part, this is true. More often than not, it is an educated guess by a local handicapper or by an employee of the track's pari-mutuel department as to what the final odds will be. At a preponderance of tracks, these guesses are far from accurate, and the predictions often fall on the high side of what the final odds actually are. This discrepancy is not due to the incompetence of the line maker but rather to the irrational and rational players who make odds inefficient.

However, the morning line can offer a fairly good idea of which horses are thought to be contenders. Let's look at the morning line for the seventh race at Finger Lakes on November 1, 2004. It was an allowance race for three-year olds and up, run at one mile and seventy yards.

NAME	MORNING LINE ODDS
Kinjet	2-1
I'llruinya	5-2
Actcelerate	4-1
Run to Glory	5-1
Dr Silver Packet	5-1
Unbrakeable George	8-1
Calsby	10-1
Darnthefrost	12-1

Right now, we have two contenders, Kinjet and I'llruinya, whose odds are very close at 2-1 and 5-2. We could almost call it with a coin toss. But, what would happen if one of these two horses were scratched? The answer is the crux for our next angle for favorites.

Trainers may scratch a horse for several reasons. Certainly, their charge could be lame. They might decide to take their chances on a bigger purse at another track. Or, they may conclude the competition is too stiff. It really does not matter. The result is the same. The race that once featured two close odds contenders now features one. Thus, the remaining horse's chance for victory has dramatically improved.

So, when one of the favorites scratches, we find our spot play using these rules:

1. Only allowance races and handicap races run at a mile or more are playable. Remember that we have this rule because favorites running in allowance, handicap, and route races win more often than in other types of races.
2. The play is, of course, on the favorite.
3. Bet only if the favorite is one of the top two morning line choices, and the other choice has scratched. Otherwise, pass the race.

In the Finger Lakes race, I'llruinya ended up scratching, and Kinjet went off as the 4-5 favorite. He immediately took the lead and never looked back as he went wire to wire, winning by five and three-quarters lengths. My $56 win bet on Kinjet returned $103.60.

Sprint to Route

A sprint race is any race less than one mile and a route race is any race a mile or longer. You may have heard the expression "horses for courses." Well, there are horses for distances as well. We consider playing our sprint-to-route angle when a trainer opts to switch his or her charge from running sprint races to running route races.

Horses whose best efforts have been in route races are at a distinct disadvantage in a sprint. Although a horse seems better suited for a shorter distance, having shown early speed in most of its route races but tiring down the stretch, the handicapper must be cognizant that early speed in sprints is much faster than early speed in routes. The speedy route-to-sprint horse might not be able to match strides with a true sprinter. Conversely, a perennial stalker, or even some closers, previously unsuccessful in sprint races, may very well find the longer distance much more comfortable. Less traffic and more running room are characteristics a sprinter may find appealing in a route race. Some stalking or closing sprinter that manages to get the early lead in a route and hugs the rail often will lead the race wire to wire. An astute trainer (a trainer ranked in the top 50 percent of all trainers at the track according to win percentage) will realize this and make the appropriate change from a sprint to a route.

Here are our rules for playing a favorite moving from a sprint to a route:

1. Only allowance, handicap, and stakes races run at a mile or more are playable. Remember we have this rule because favorites running in allowance, handicap, and route races win more often than in other types of races.
2. The play is on — you guessed it — the favorite.
3. Bet only those favorites that raced in a sprint the last time out.
4. Bet only those favorites whose trainer is ranked in the top 50 percent of all trainers at the track according to his or her win percentage.

The sixth race at Meadowlands on November 5, 2004, was a fantastic opportunity to play this angle. It was the Honey Bee Stakes, a mile and one-sixteenth route for three-year-old fillies.

NAME	LAST DIST.	POST TIME ODDS	TRAINER	WIN %	11/05/04 FINISH
Emerald Earrings	6f	1-1 Favorite	Alexander	28	1st
Richetta	1 1/16 Mi.	5-2	Graham	10	2nd
Ensenada	1 Mile	6-1	Goldberg	17	6th
Diavla	1 Mi. 70yd	7-1	Dowd	15	4th
Freeroll	1 Mi. 70yd	10-1	Hennig	14	5th
From Away	1 Mi. 70yd	6-1	Matz	15	3rd

One does not see many setups like this one, and I chose to double the size of my bet and place one hundred dollars to win on Emerald Earrings. She won by three and three-quarters lengths and returned $220 for my effort.

It takes only one winning angle to make your trip to the track a profitable one. Again, choose an angle you like and stick with it. We have seen that some of the rules can be interchanged among the different methods. In fact, from these angles may spring an entirely new approach.

In the next chapter we will talk a little bit about progressive betting and how to apply it to both the longshot and favorite methods. We will again discuss the allocator, a player who hedges his or her bets, and detail a money management system that can be used successfully when you are playing the longshots. But first, here is a list of tracks you may find helpful in locating races that lend themselves to your particular style of play. If your local track does not make the category that best suits your betting style, it may well be worth it to sign up for an online service that allows you to bet at most tracks across the country.

AGGRESSIVE/ LONGSHOTS	CONSERVATIVE/ FAVORITES	MODERATE/ MIXED
Calder	Aqueduct	Arlington
Canterbury	Belmont	Delaware
Colonial Downs	Churchill Downs	Ellis Park
Emerald Downs	Del Mar	Fair Grounds
Fort Erie	Gulfstream	Fairplex
Hawthorne	Hollywood	Golden Gate
Louisiana Downs	Keeneland	Hialeah
Meadowlands	Santa Anita	Laurel
Mountaineer	Saratoga	Lone Star
Philadelphia		Monmouth
Pleasanton Fair		Oaklawn
Prairie Meadows		Pimlico
Remington		Turfway
River Downs		
Rockingham		
Sam Houston		
Santa Rosa Fair		
Solano Fair		
Sportsman's		
Stockton Fair		
Suffolk Downs		
Thistledown		
Turf Paradise		

If you cannot locate your track on this list, assume that it falls into the aggressive/longshot category. Playing multiple tracks is a good way to increase your betting action, if so desired.

6

Money Management

Diversifying investments offers protection against wild market fluctuations. By selecting among different stocks in different industries in different sectors, you can eliminate the risk associated with any one company's or one sector's bad fortune. However, over-diversification is possible. Investing in too many companies may reduce the overall return of your investment portfolio.

In chapter two I said that allocators hedge their bets by making other bets to offset their risk. Conservative allocators may feel more comfortable with less risk and prefer not to offset their bets by dutching. If they are not averse to risk, offsetting their bets may increase their profitability by reducing losses attributable to unexpected outcomes.

There are several betting methods, but for our purposes we will discuss progressive betting and dutching, or diversification.

Progressions

Progressive betting, unlike flat betting (where the bettor wagers the same amount on each race regardless of how the day is going), requires the bettor to increase the amount of every bet subsequent to each loss. For example, in a typical Martingale progression, the oldest known negative progression system, a handicapper betting five units (one unit equaling the basic two-dollar bet) would bet ten dollars on her first bet, and if she lost, bet twenty dollars on her second bet, and if she lost yet again, forty dollars on her third bet and so on, doubling her wager after each loss until she won, then resume by placing another ten-dollar bet. Progressive betting is superior to flat betting in that if we flat bet every race, in the long run we would find we were cashing tickets on favorites more than on long-shots, so our bankroll would eventually disappear. Also, the track take, or "house-advantage," would expedite this process.

The logic behind progressive betting is that eventually the handicapper will be "due to win." For example, if bettors used the Martingale progressive system, they would simply double their bet after each loss, assuming that their luck would soon change and they would cash in on a large bet, thereby recouping their previous losses as well as a decent profit. The main drawback of progressive betting is that horseplayers can quickly reach the point of diminishing returns, beyond which lies the demise of their bankroll.

Therefore, we must devise a progression that can withstand a long run of losses and fully exploit a selection method that yields frequent winners.

The aggressive, longshot approaches are susceptible to long series of losses. However, they enjoy a higher payoff per win. So, it is suggested that these races be either flat bet or progressively bet with an extremely gradual progression such as the Fibonacci Sequence. The Fibonacci Sequence begins with 1, and each number that follows it is the sum of the previous two numbers so, (0+1) 1, (1+1) 2, (1+2) 3, (2+3) 5, (3+5) 8, (5+8) 13, (8+13) 21, (13+21) 34 ... to infinity. To us professionals, these numbers are "base units" so 1-2-3-5 would translate into two-dollar, four-dollar, six-dollar, and ten-dollar bets. (The professional handicapper is welcome to use any multiple of the base units with which he or she feels comfortable.) Personally, I am not a big fan of progressive betting in general, but the Fibonacci Sequence is certainly my favorite method as it is the basis for technical investing, which involves the analysis of chart patterns and trading volumes to identify promising buy and sell signals.

The conservative, favorite methods are characterized by frequent wins but at a lower payoff per win. Flat betting works but does not take full advantage of this situation. Consequently, an accelerated progression such as betting base units of 1-4-6-12 (two dollars, eight dollars, twelve dollars, and twenty-four dollars) works best. You'll see that our initial bet is higher according to our probability of winning and graduates much more steeply after a loss because of our expected lower payoff. That sequence is just a suggestion. You may find a sequence that works better for you, or you may opt for the dutching method.

Dutching

Dutching is the professional handicapper's equivalent to portfolio diversification. One of the greatest mistakes an investor can make is not properly diversifying his or her portfolio. Adequate diversification will include an increased number of investments, allowing those with upward price movements to offset those with downward price movements.

In handicapping, dutching allows a bettor to wager on two or more runners, at different odds, in the same race. The bets are made in proportion to each horse's chance of winning, so that no matter which runner prevails, the payoff will be the same. Since dutching allows us to bet on three or four runners, obviously we have a better chance of cashing more tickets. However, even when we win while dutching, we will always have some losing tickets with this method.

Here is how it works: Assume that through applying a long-shot angle, you have eliminated the non-contenders and are left with three horses. You are confident one of the three will be victorious but have no particular bias toward any of them. The rule concerning ties thus far has been very clear: Bet the horse with the highest post-time odds. However, there is an alternative. By placing a varying win bet on each of the three horses, the dollar amounts being dictated by the odds, you will realize a profit no matter which of the three wins. In addition, the profit will be approximately the same for each outcome, and you can predetermine it.

So, how do we know how much to wager on each horse in order to guarantee a profit? First, we need to convert the horse's current odds into a percentage. This tells us what the market or pool says is the real-time percent chance each horse has of winning the race. Doing this is very simple. Just add one to the horse's current odds and divide the sum into 100. For example, a horse at odds of 9-1 tells us that the collective thinking of all handicappers has put a 10 percent chance of winning [100/(1+9)] on this horse. (In cases where the formula does not produce an even number, round your answer to the nearest whole number.)

Next, we assign a unit value (based on one's personal preference or risk tolerance) to each percentage point. Although the value assigned is entirely at each individual handicapper's discretion, it must be the same for each horse. This is also how we are able to predetermine our profit. In the above example, we could assign ten cents, one dollar, five dollars, etc., to each percentage point. Assigning a twenty-cent unit would have us wagering two dollars on this horse to win.

Adding two more contenders with current odds of 3-1 and 4-1, we find that the market or pool says that the real-time percent chances of winning are 25 percent and 20 percent respectively: [100/(1+3)]=25 and [100/(1+4)]=20. The chart below shows how we would fare if any of our three horses won.

ODDS	%	AMOUNT BET	WIN PAYOFF
3-1	25	$5.00	$20.00
4-1	20	$4.00	$20.00
9-1	10	$2.00	$20.00

With a total outlay of only eleven dollars, we would expect a profit of nine dollars no matter which of our horses won. A profit of $90 would require a total outlay of $110. Note that we are betting more in proportion to a horse's chance of winning.

Some companies offer dutching software and hand-held computers that can make these computations, but I find that when I go to the track, it is just as easy to carry a wallet-sized version of the chart below.

ODDS	%	ODDS	%	ODDS	%
1-5	83	2-1	33	10-1	9
2-5	71	5-2	29	11-1	8
1-2	67	3-1	25	12-1	8
3-5	62	7-2	22	13-1	7
4-5	56	4-1	20	14-1	7
1-1	50	9-2	18	15-1	6
6-5	45	5-1	17	18-1	5
7-5	42	6-1	14	25-1	4
3-2	40	7-1	12	30-1	3
8-5	38	8-1	11	40-1	2
9-5	36	9-1	10	70-1	1

Notice that the odds as low as 5-2 are in bold. This is to mark the point separating sufficient profit from meager profit or, in some instances, loss because the payout for horses whose odds are lower than 5-2 just is not enough to generate an adequate profit. In some cases we actually would suffer losses. I use the same reasoning when limiting the number of horses played, as we are reaching the point of diminishing returns when we try to dutch four or five horses.

The conservative/favorite methods offer us a chance to modify the dutching method a bit. Remember that there is no such thing as a tie when we apply the conservative/favorite methods.

The bet is always on the favorite or there is no bet at all. However, we can, in lieu of using an accelerated progression or a flat-betting strategy, make our wagers on favorites according to the horse's percentage chance of winning. For example, if the favorite has post time odds of 7-5, and we have assigned a unit value of one dollar per percentage point, we bet forty-two dollars because, according to the chart, a 7-5 choice has a 42 percent chance of winning. If our next favorite selection has post time odds of 3-5, we wager sixty-two dollars. Again, the unit value per percentage point is entirely up to each individual but must remain constant.

As with the stock market, there is a certain degree of volatility in the betting pool. It is not at all uncommon to see sizable fluctuations in the odds, especially at smaller tracks. To compensate for these fluctuations, one should endeavor to wait until the last possible second to place a wager. Consequently, the most accurate, up-to-date information will be used to make the calculations.

The dutching technique can also be applied to exotic wagers such as the daily double or exacta. Personally, I prefer to pass on the doubles as the fields usually consist of cheaper, less-consistent horses. However, I often employ this method in exacta play for several reasons. First, exacta odds are higher, thus giving bettors the capability to dutch more combinations without reaching the point of diminishing returns. Second, exacta odds do not fluctuate to the degree the odds of a single horse will because there are far more combinations to bet than just eight or ten horses. This allows us time enough to place our wagers without the added worry of being shut out at the ticket window.

When dutching exactas, use the same odds/percentage figures shown in the table on page 73. Calculating the odds by hand is much more tedious; however, most tracks have television monitors that display the odds for all possible combinations. If not, I suggest investing in a hand-held device. In the next chapter, though, I will show you how to calculate the figures by hand.

Armed with this knowledge about odds and percentages, you should no longer simply straight box exacta combinations. Remember that we want to bet more in proportion to a horse's, or an exacta combination's, chance of winning. For example, let us assume that the odds of the A-B combination are 3-1 while the odds of the B-A combination are 4-1. Also remember the A-B combination of 3-1 translates to a 25 percent chance of winning and the B-A combination at 4-1, to a 20 percent chance of winning. If we assign a one-dollar unit per percentage point, we would wager twenty-five dollars on the A-B exacta but only twenty dollars on the B-A exacta. Either way the exacta comes in, our total return is one hundred dollars. Subtracting the total outlay of forty-five dollars, we realize a profit of fifty-five dollars. We will analyze the exacta bet in greater detail in the next chapter.

In summary, here are the advantages and guidelines for dutching horses and exacta combinations:

ADVANTAGES:
1. Bettor's risk spread over two or more wagers.
2. Profits regardless of which wager wins.
3. Profit approximately the same for each outcome.
4. Profit predetermined.
5. Bets directly proportional to a selection's chance of winning.

GUIDELINES:
1. Bet only dutch selections offering odds of 5-2 or higher.
2. Except for exacta wagering, do not dutch more than three selections.
3. Place bets only on the favorites, but the amount bet is in

direct proportion to a selection's chance of winning.

4. Wait until the last possible second to place your wagers.

5. Avoid dutching the early or late doubles.

6. Do not straight box exactas.

It would be a huge mistake not to include this proven money management technique in your arsenal. You would not invest your life savings in only one stock, so why bet only one horse? Dutching will have you cashing more tickets at the window, and it will assist you in achieving your daily, monthly, and yearly profit objectives in a very effective and efficient manner. Add it to your toolbox, and I am sure you will have as much success with it as I have.

7

Finding Value in Exactas

Though many handicappers strictly adhere to the adage "do not bet the exacta; play only to win," horseplayers can find value in exactas by understanding a basic mathematical equation as well as the psychological profiles of the players.

Many players believe the exacta is a gimmick invented to separate a fool from his money. Most handicappers will cite the higher takeout percentage as a reason not to play exactas, explaining that exacta bettors reap less per wagered dollar than skillful win bettors. Other, more imaginative, players believe the high exacta payoffs encourage dishonesty. They reason that every time a longshot combination comes in and the payoff is lower than expected, insiders have engineered a betting coup and sent in heavy money.

Betting the exacta involves some small risks, but there are ways to reduce those risks. One bettor could miss the second-place finisher but easily protect herself by backing up her first choice with a win bet. Betting an exacta underlay is another risk. But, with the use of television monitors and a calculator, the savvy bettor can eliminate that risk as well.

A few years ago I pored through the results of 1,165 races from Aqueduct, Laurel Park, Suffolk Downs, Gulfstream Park, Fair Grounds, Bay Meadows, and Santa Anita. Using the final odds, I calculated the expected exacta payoff for each race and compared it to the actual payoff. I found not only that the exacta can be a good bet, but it is so most of the time. Interestingly enough, the results also show that longshot combinations do tend to produce lower-than-expected payoffs, though it is doubtful that this is a result of collusion.

Before we go further, let us take a quick course on how to

calculate the odds from the win pool in order to compare them to exacta payoffs. This will help us determine which exacta plays are probable underlays and probable overlays.

First, calculate the odds percentage for each of the two horses you are considering. Refer to the last chapter to review how to accomplish this. Then, multiply both percentages together. For example, if the first horse is at 7-2, its odds percentage would be 22.22. We do not do any rounding up or down at this point as we did in the last chapter when we were simply looking for an amount to wager. In this case, we are looking for an expected payoff on a two-horse combination. Amounts to wager and expected payoffs are apples and oranges. Likewise, if the second horse is at 9-1, its odds percentage would be 10. So, 22.22 multiplied by 10 equals 222.20. Lastly, divide the product (222.20) by 100 less the odds percentage of the first horse [222.20/(100-22.22)] equals 2.87.

Now, check the probable exacta payoff for combinations shown on the television monitor at the racetrack. Our last bit of math is to divide 200 by 2.87 for an expected payoff of $69.69 based on a $2 ticket (adjust downward to account for breakage and takeout). If payoffs are based on a one-dollar ticket, divide 100 by 2.87 for an expected payoff of $34.84. Comparing the probable payoffs shown on the television monitor against our expected payoffs using the win pool odds should guide us in determining whether our chosen exacta combination is an overlay or underlay.

As mentioned earlier, the exacta appears to be a good bet the majority of the time. Of the 1,165 races examined, the expected exacta payoff was less than the actual payoff 980 times. This means that the exacta was an overlay 84.1 percent of the time. Conversely, it was an underlay only 15.9 percent of the time.

Reviewing the results of those 1,165 races shows it became a somewhat simple matter to predict which races were more likely to produce overlays and which were likely to be underlays. Studying the sample of overlays, I found the favorite ran first or second 650 times or 66.3 percent of the time. Favorites ran first or second only forty times (21.6 percent) when the exacta produced an underlay.

The reason for the high percentage of overlays is probably twofold. For one, too many people subscribe to the aforementioned mantra, "do not bet the exacta; bet only to win." Second, the non-professionals tend to overbet the favorite. Too many people doing the same thing in a market or betting pool leads to inefficiencies in other sectors of the market.

Again, two forces are working simultaneously. Those two forces account for the very low percentage of favorites involved in producing an exacta underlay. If favorites are being overbet, thus leaving value in other prospects, it can be expected that the exacta payoffs for these longer-odds combinations will be inefficiently priced. By examining the psychology of the irrational handicapper, we can surmise that his primary motive behind purchasing an exacta ticket is greed. The lure of a huge payoff entices bettors to purchase exacta tickets on combinations of longer-odds horses. This drives the actual exacta payoffs for horses with longer odds lower than expected.

Playing the exacta is a viable alternative to betting the conservative/favorite selections to win. If you can uncover a very sound second choice, it may be worthwhile to play both in an exacta combination. If not, do not pass on playing the favorite. Clearly, you should not deviate from the rules set forth in the aggressive/longshot methods unless you ignore the rule governing ties and dutch several selections.

Above all, remember that handicapping is an art, not a science. When devising any system, method, or betting strategy, you should be sure to leave room to maneuver. Absolute rules can preclude many opportunities.

Down the Stretch We Come

Handicapping *the Wall Street Way* has shown that there are, indeed, many similarities between the stock market and the pari-mutuel betting pool. The flaws that exist with both the efficient market and efficient pool hypotheses can be exploited with simple strategies such as eliminating the Triple Crown contender in his bid for the last jewel, the Belmont Stakes. More detailed methods can be used to find contenders with unfavorable data (e.g., one coming back from a layoff). We know that these layoff horses are largely overlooked because of blind faith in outdated beliefs. Horses that are overlooked for one reason or another create inefficiencies, thus potential for profit for the professional handicapper.

We now know that there are three major types of horse-players, as well as two minor ones. Each type is motivated to bet by different goals, and to further their efforts, they will gravitate toward different types of races. A questionnaire was included to help assist you in determining what type of player you are and what strategies might be best suited for you.

These strategies were reviewed in detail and several winning angles for each style of play were discussed. A list of tracks most likely to offer races for each style of wagering was included. In addition, we explored the topic of money management, examining the advantages and disadvantages of progressive betting systems. Revisiting the topic of risk management led us to study a successful money management system designed to spread risk.

I sincerely hope that this book proves to be a very sound investment. Pride is another emotion that drives people to make certain decisions, and I can honestly say that I take a great deal of pride in *Handicapping the Wall Street Way*. I would not have put my name on it if I did not think it could prove profitable to the reader. Remember: always think independently of the crowd; bet what others cannot or are afraid to bet, and you will prosper.

Glossary

Allowance race — This is the third level of competition after maiden and claiming races. The conditions of eligibility are similar to those of a claiming race, but the horses are not for sale.

Bay — Brown horse with black mane and tail.

Box — A bet on two or more horses in a race that covers all combinations.

Break — The start of a race.

Breakage — After the payoff, pennies that are left over are rounded off to a nickel or dime.

Bullet — The best work for that distance on a given day. This is signified by a black dot.

Checked — When a jockey has to pull up a horse momentarily because of traffic trouble.

Claiming race — A race that sets a price for which any horse in the race may be purchased. Different claiming prices signify different class levels. It is the most common of all races. This is the second level of competition after maidens.

Clockers — Timers of workouts.

Close — To gain ground on leaders toward the end of the race.

Colt — An entire male horse less than five years old.

Condition — Refers to the fitness of a horse; also, refers to the details of a race, such as type, distance, age, sex.

Connections — Owner, trainer, and others with an interest in a horse.

Contrarian thinking — Believing that the improbable will probably happen.

Daily double — A bet requiring one to select the winners of any two designated races.

Drop down — A horse racing against a lower class of horses than it previously had been.

Dueler — A horse that is on the lead by less than a length or within one length.

Dutch — To spread one's risk among two or more wagers.

Exacta — A type of combination bet requiring one to select the winner and second-place finisher of a race.

Filly — An unbred female horse less than five years old.

Foal — A newborn horse.

Front-runner — A horse that prefers to run on the lead rather than come from behind.

Furlong — An eighth of a mile.

Gelding — A male horse that has been castrated.

Handicap race — A race in which the racing secretary has assigned weights to the entries after evaluating the horses' past performances. This is the fourth level of competition after maiden, claiming, and allowance races.

Handicapper — One who makes selections based on past performances.

Handily — An easy victory or workout, without any urging from the rider.

Horse — For purposes of this book, the term "horse" has been generically used, otherwise, an entire male horse five years old or older.

In the money — A first-, second-, or third-place finish.

Maiden race — A race for horses that have never won a race. A horse "breaks its maiden" by winning and moving up into another race category. This is the first level of competition.

Mare — A female horse five years old or older.

Morning line — A track employee's, or local handicapper's, best guess at what the post time odds will be.

Overlay — A horse whose odds during real-time wagering are higher than the morning line. This horse is usually undervalued by the betting public.

Payoff — Amount each bettor receives for a winning ticket, based on a $1 or $2 purchase.

Place — A second-place finish in a race; also, a straight bet in which a horse must finish first or second for the bettor to cash a ticket.

Pool — A total amount bet to win, place, show, or in combination betting.

Save ground — Used to describe horse that runs the shortest amount of distance, near the rail.

Scratch — To withdraw a horse from a race.

Send — To enter a horse and try to win the race.

Send it in — Bet heavily to win.

Show — A third-place finish in a race; also, a straight bet in which the bettor cashes the ticket if the horse finishes first, second, or third.

Smart money — Bets made by insiders or professional handicappers.

Speed ball — A horse that leads by more than one length in fast fractions.

Spot play — Wagering only on exceptionally playable races and horses.

Stakes race — This is the highest level of competition. Owners pay an entry fee to nominate, enter, and run their horses.

Stalker — A horse that runs between one and four lengths behind the leader.

Stride — The amount of ground a horse covers after each foot has landed on the ground.

Takeout — The percentage of tax taken from each betting pool at the track.

Tote board — Computerized machine that records bets as they are made and calculates odds.

Triple crown — An honorary award to the three-year-old that wins the Kentucky Derby, Preakness Stakes, and Belmont Stakes.

Underlay — A horse whose odds during real time wagering are lower than the morning line. This horse is usually overvalued by the betting public.

Win — A first-place finish in a race; also, a straight bet in which a horse must finish first for a person to cash a ticket.

Mark E. Ripple

Mark E. Ripple first became interested in racing when as a teenager his family moved to Saratoga Springs, New York. Though he initially played only harness races, he became increasingly interested in Thoroughbreds.

Ripple left college early to become a stockbroker and worked for such firms as Merrill Lynch and Prudential-Bache Securities. His experience as a stockbroker opened his eyes to a new way to approach handicapping and thus the seeds for *Handicapping the Wall Street Way: Picking Xtra Winners at the Track* were sewn.

Ripple, who has written articles for *American Turf Monthly*, continues to trade stocks when he is not studying handicapping. He is married and lives near Saratoga Springs.

Ripple can be reached via e-mail at: xtrawinners@hotmail.com.